NISHA PATEL

FOR THE RECORD

a poem

ARSENAL PULP PRESS
VANCOUVER

FOR THE RECORD

ARSENAL PULP PRESS
Suite 202 – 211 East Georgia St.
Vancouver, BC V6A 1Z6
Canada
arsenalpulp.com

The publisher gratefully acknowledges the support of the Canada Council for the Arts and the British Columbia Arts Council for its publishing program and the Government of Canada and the Government of British Columbia (through the Book Publishing Tax Credit Program) for its publishing activities.

BRITISH COLUMBIA | BRITISH COLUMBIA ARTS COUNCIL An agency of the Province of British Columbia
Canada Council for the Arts Conseil des arts du Canada
Canada

Arsenal Pulp Press acknowledges the xʷməθkʷəy̓əm (Musqueam), Sḵwx̱wú7mesh (Squamish), and səlilwətaɬ (Tsleil-Waututh) Nations, custodians of the traditional, ancestral, and unceded territories where our office is located. We pay respect to their histories, traditions, and continuous living cultures and commit to accountability, respectful relations, and friendship.

Arsenal Pulp Press is committed to reducing the consumption of non-renewable resources in the making of our books wherever possible. We make every effort to use materials that support a sustainable future.

EU Safety Regulations authorized representative: Easy Access System Europe, Mustamäe tee 50, 10621 Tallinn, Estonia, gpsr.requests@easproject.com.

Cover and text design by Rebecca Poulin
Cover art by Rebecca Poulin
Edited by Katherine Abbass
Copy-edited by JC Cham
Proofread by Alison Strobel

Printed and bound in Canada

Library and Archives Canada Cataloguing in Publication:
Title: For the record : a poem / Nisha Patel.
Names: Patel, Nisha, 1992– author.
Identifiers: Canadiana (print) 20260130060 | Canadiana (ebook) 2026013466X |
ISBN 9781834050508 (softcover) | ISBN 9781834050515 (EPUB)
Subjects: LCGFT: Poetry.
Classification: LCC PS8631.A82945 F67 2026 | DDC C811/.6—dc23

ADVANCE PRAISE FOR *For the Record*

"Nisha Patel's *For the Record* meets the enormity of the historical present with grace and erudition and emotional clarity. The book asks, What is poetry in the face of a pandemic, in the face of climate disaster, in the face of genocide? *For the Record* is a record of a long and complex moment that we are fortunate to have now and will be fortunate to have in the future."

—BILLY-RAY BELCOURT, author of *The Idea of an Entire Life*

"Like a Formula 1 car ripping around the track at 350 km/hr, Nisha takes the reader on a poetic narrative journey that brings us back to the vestiges of 2020 COVID and into the present. This poem blurs together just like how the grandstands would look to an F1 driver to give the reader a sense of despair over government inadequacy but also show the way that we move forward individually and as a community through trying times."

—CONOR KERR, author of *Beaver Hills Forever*

"This is not a time capsule, nor an archive, nor a memoir. While much of the world speaks of COVID-19 in the past tense, *For the Record* demands we reckon with the ongoing presence of the virus and the systemic injustices it lays bare. In this powerful work, Patel interweaves years' worth of news headlines with the intimacies of the ill body, collapsing time and space in an urgent act of witnessing."

—JENNIFER BOWERING DELISLE, author of *Stock*

"From piercing indictments of organized abandonment to tender elegies for her masi as the poet becomes one herself, Nisha Patel unfurls a sense of presence to our unending pandemic times. Her attention to the world is a welcome balm to the gleaming surfaces of colonial racial capital forcing us to forget; despite the speed of tragedy, this poem demands that we slow down and pay attention to love."

—JANE SHI, author of *echolalia echolalia*

"Nisha Patel's *For the Record* examines part of the COVID-19 pandemic with a journalist's eye and a poet's heart. Her poems amplify the stories of the marginalized and their struggles and tell the larger story of COVID-19 while weaving in her own personal health issues. *For the Record* is an example of the personal and the political beautifully intertwined."

—ALEXIS KIENLEN, poet, journalist, and novelist

THIS POEM IS ALIVE.
615 ALBERTANS WHO HAD COVID-19 ARE NOT.
AS MORE DIE, THE POEM WILL GROW.[1]

—Alex Antoneshyn, *CTV News*,
December 7, 2020

CONTENTS

"I Am So, So Sad": Husband, Friends of Cargill Worker
Who Died from COVID-19 Honour Her in Memorial [2]
High River Cargill Workers Being Neglected PPE Equipment
amid COVID-19 Outbreak [3]
Canada's Victims of Flight PS752 [4]

when 2020's Ukraine Airlines flight PS752 goes down
the City of Edmonton asks me to write about it
to hold my face to the clouds until the edges blur
and sing to grief and tragedy of lovely people
disappearing in a blush of sunrise

Iran, a nation of words,
and none of them asked to speak first
expected to nod at the vigils, burn fingertips on candle flame
mourn wide for all the news stations to get a good story

when the City asked me to write about it
I told them the truth:
that I would rather have pulled out my tongue
like my mother pulls weeds
before burying someone else's story with my sorrow
would rather have the sunburns back
from all the summers I spent scrunching stems in fist
breath blowing ripe dandelion seeds
into the wind

but here we are again
asking muddy bodies to write about
            love, not anger
            hope, not fear
as if we can choose not to write about politics
as if any of us can afford the difference

the real currency of a pandemic

is how much you get to talk about anything else

so I write about my mother
working for companies building pipelines
and how it is as good a job as any
when raising four kids

I write about my father
indiscriminate in his attention, his care for
the crashed carcasses of cars in his auto-body yard
unbattered by the news of death and dying
as it is the living who still need his
time

he does not ask where the white trucks are going
even as they ooze their wheels down the High Level Bridge
from Jasper Ave to 109 Street
from Calgary Trail to Calgary
as they Convoy for Freedom

and I can't count how many Members of the Legislative Assembly of Alberta
will not remember the name of the first worker to die from COVID-19
despite how often they'll wash their hands of her

Hiep Bui, picking bones from beef
how her name will join the nameless on the Cargill kill floor

how essential the temporary have become
how foreign the ghosts will be
when all that's left are the fully packed trays of Cargill beef
gracing the refrigerators of Albertans
stuck at home

I didn't believe in revenge before I learnt
only the managers got the masks

but some bosses are used to this
leaving waves of white in their wake
and waking to the week's quotas without question

and Hiep Bui, you were everyone's auntie
pockets full for twenty-four years
with tightly wound foil wrappers
never anything less
Hiep Bui, I know what language you speak
Hiep Bui, I too come from lands of stomach and belly
we who do not wait for children to die in the labour of adult bodies
before we bring them sweets

you deserve more than this poem
and much more than a headline

and somewhere my father returns to work
gold Werther's wrapper in hand
and he says your name

and my mother in her home bends her head over the pressure cooker's steam
waiting for her daughter to call
and she says your name

I lie down in my bed
underneath the covers and the guilt
an immigrant's daughter who stays home
condemned to quarantine and the writing of poems
and I say your name, Hiep Bui

I keep it close to teeth and gum
so when they ask me not to write about politics
they will have to yank each tooth one by one
until I spill you into the sun

595 words

Hamilton Seals Historic 7th Title
with Peerless Wet-Weather Victory in Turkey [5]
COVID-19 Restrictions Putting Out the Light of Diwali in Edmonton [6]
How COVID-19 Overwhelmed Canada's Long-Term Care System [7]

Alberta reports 1,000 new COVID cases
the day Lewis Hamilton wins his 7th Formula 1 World Drivers' Championship

my mother cancels Diwali
my masi goes to work at the nursing home
the 270th day in a row

I rearrange the furniture
buy more lamps
and a webcam
carve a hole to thread an ethernet cable
through fifty-year-old walk-up walls
with nothing but impatience
and a butterknife

like time
this knife has new purpose

COVID-19: Nurses May Be Recalled as ICUs, ERs in Edmonton and South Zone Under Pressure, Alberta's Hospitalizations Pass 200 [8]
COVID-19: Staff at Calgary Hospitals Told to "Engage in Oxygen Conservation" as Cases Rise [9]
How Alberta's COVID-19 Crisis Became "Absolutely Frightening" [10]

my friend is recalled to the medical floor she left years ago
trades her favourite coats and cashmere
for scrubs and surgical blues
she has practised injecting needles on oranges
and bedside nursing is no longer optional

fear balloons around her throat
like a blood pressure cuff left too long
a tourniquet tied and forgotten

time is reported, monitored, and measured
mechanized deep breathing
the hiss of piston and pump
splashes of bleach and isopropyl alcohol and steam
staining walls the colour of old milk

a loudspeaker booms, floors flooded with fissured light
flashing codes in spills and shudders

round corners, patients corner nurses
asking for pain relief and reassurance
eyes take in the language of alarm
the blood and veins and plasma
bouncing off the backs of corneas
faster than eyes are shut

as oxygen masks run out
visitation is limited to the ghosts

when I develop type 2 diabetes
I learn that modern medicine is an expensive miracle
blood-glucose monitors are copaid privileges
that my body requires special authorization
to benefit

my body is reluctant to give
sugar to the wastewater
glucose to my bloodstream
hormones to quench my hunger
pooling until sick and sticky through my veins

glucose wets and slows me

between throwing up and passing out
I write grants, host livestreams
I stay awake until my body overheats
not sure if rationing insulin or poetry would kill me faster

Aritzia Weathers the COVID-19 Storm with Increase in E-Commerce Sales[11]
Opinion: Sephora Never Valued Workers Like Me[12]
No End to COVID-19 Webcam Shortage[13]

Aritzia's online sales are through the roof
free returns are standard now
as is hand sanitizer
carrying pulse oximeters
COVID tests in the glovebox
surgical masks dangling on the rear-view mirror

my friend comes home from the hospital floor
soothes herself with a credit card and cha
warmth in the face of weariness and weather

Sephora underpays their workers
but I still order eyeshadow, new brushes, creme blush, and glitter
to pay the bills—a return on investment because looking good
is currency even at 91 megabytes per second

luckily wigs and glue cost less than a dye job
and in 720 pixels there is hardly any difference

F1 Confirm 2020 Azerbaijan, Singapore and Japanese Grands Prix Have Been Cancelled [14]
5 Steps F1 Is Taking to Ensure Racing Is as Safe as Possible When the 2020 Season Starts [15]
F1 Will Not Cancel Races If a Driver Tests Positive for COVID-19 [16]

the Chinese Grand Prix is cancelled
    then Vietnam
    Singapore
    Japan
    Australia closes her borders

Formula 1 racing compromises
too much money at stake to leave
    beasts
    and men
    and machinery
in the garages

too many aspiring boys
giving their childhoods
and bones
and bodies
to motorsport

    too many celebrities left bored
    and off-camera

Romain Grosjean's "Life Saved" by Halo After Remarkable Escape at Bahrain GP [17]
Calgary Police and Anti-Mask Protesters Clash at Weekend Protests; Alberta Surpasses 90,000 COVID-19 Cases [18]

Italy mourns
unmitigated COVID seething within her
one of the highest deaths per capita

newspapers blame Italians' social natures
the young who live with their elders
and their elders who live too long

Ferrari, the red heart of racing, protest
quarantined families and staff
unable to service and build the container
for these boys to shutter their dreams in

but fans are mad that audiences are illegal gatherers

I remember seeing the smallest of coffins in 2016
learned that Italy was earthquake prone

reports now reveal negligence
a failure to comply with seismic retrofit regulations

I know now that the colour of the wood encasing a childhood is white
same as a signal for a slow car ahead
and that the heart of the child and the country is red

Romain Grosjean lives through a crash through a barrier that splits his car
in half
flames lighting fuel and fuel feeding flames
I couldn't understand how anyone in F1 had opposed the halo

but when anti-mask protesters insist on sneering at the steps of the Legislature
the same week that twenty-six people died in isolation
I learn that the real currency of a pandemic
is how much you get to risk your life without hurting anyone else

How 2020 Changed Lewis Hamilton[19]
Evidence Suggests SARS-CoV-2 Spike Protein Can Enter the Brain[20]

a week after Lewis wins seven F1 World Drivers' Championships
he contracts COVID

his victory is a persistent miracle
predictable yet still momentous
he misses a race
returns faster

the pinnacle of motorsport

COVID cases spike across Canada
Alberta is a reservoir of sickness leaking into groundwater

we will learn that COVID crosses the blood-brain barrier
splits our cells, like our citizens, in half

and maybe the cost of crossing the checkered flag means
accepting that you love something so much it could kill you

but we're playing pretend with time's promises
waiting for the track to clear
and hoping
we all come home

"The Whole World Is My Karaoke Machine": Singing Mailman Brings Smiles to Edmonton Streets[21]

the Canada Post mailman sings up and down my street
delivering my tenth package in two weeks

ginseng supplements and cinnamon
mangrove tree seeds from France and Florida

I go online like I am going outside
plant the mangroves in the sway of my new aquarium
still don't believe a tree can grow in salt and freshwater alike

I wonder if he is taking his vitamins
nettle leaf and nattokinase
lions' mane and turmeric
melatonin for sleep

I listen to his footfalls
the metal of my mail slot an open palm waiting for a handshake
in the form of a constituency letter or donation solicitation
or internet bill
his voice, proof of something
my imagination never dreamt of needing

I am learning to play the piano

***Kenney Quiet on Protesters After Issuing COVID-19 "Wake Up Call" to South Asian Community*[22]**
***Opinion: Stop Stigmatizing South Asians for High Infection Rates*[23]**
***Kenney's "Wake-Up Call" to Northeast Calgary Condemned as "Scapegoating"*[24]**

Premier Jason Kenney tells RED FM to wake up
to their caseload, their burden, their culpability
my people, berated over our own South Asian radio station
a man with a mouth, shoes on in my living room
an earworm of doubt and guilt
a sound bite speaking in the stillness of the drive to the night shift
opening the airwaves to spit and spread blame

while the spread of death and dying in care homes, camps, and cruises
all the fault of people like me
all the fault of Northeast Calgarians
who live just like Southeast Edmontonians
(who live just like Italians)

all the fault of South Asians stretching generations, residency permits
basement apartments, minimum wages
trading dollars for cents, slums for slumlords, goons for government
only to get government for goons
again

but it is not Jason Kenney's government at fault
not when he's done his part by cancelling Diwali
and leaving schools unventilated
and long-term care underfunded

my community, treated like an infestation, my culture infectious
a strain on the systems they let strain through constant cuts
the systems in question
still hiring cleaners, drivers, doctors, nurses, and janitors

to clean the mud from his boots
in my living room

he means to say

          COVID is the problem

                    COVID splinters families

                              Indians need to wake up because

                    COVID steals joy, not the health budget

          COVID is the enemy, not shrinking wages

COVID stole this country, his country, his surplus, his oil, because

COVID, not conservatism, is the disease without cure
a problem shaped like a punch clock at the Cargill meat-packing plant
the only numbers he can read come in multiples of four
and this is no election year

he asks Indians to wake up, care less about our families
because Diwali is cancelled but we'll be free for Christmas
and at Christmas isolation pods and ten-person bubbles will surface
I have an overflowing bathtub of family by this metric
we'd rather be alone than leave anyone circling the drain

so the Indians work
slaughter the turkeys
pick the cranberries
fix the cars
restock the Kraft Dinner

one of my masis delivers Boxing Day flyers
my mother works online from her basement
hopes the oil sands will not run dry
before her mortgage payments

neither our citizenship nor our work ethic protect us

From Books to Beer, COVID-19 Sparks Delivery Boom in Alberta [25]
Alberta Takes Steps to Ease Regulatory Burden on Truck Drivers During COVID-19 Response [26]
How Delivery Drivers Became Vital in the Pandemic [27]

citizens rely on Uber Eats, DoorDash orders
skip dishes delivered by dads and moms and immigrants
toilet paper and meat run low at Loblaws
even though Korean grocers and Asian supermarkets overflow

ice cream cones become deliverable
soup becomes deliverable
Caesar salad goes up in price
loses the anchovies
the bacon
the plastic bags
and becomes deliverable

neighbours watch neighbours order Starbucks
after getting out of bed at 2 p.m.

neighbours leave the house
come too close to other neighbours
and other neighbours' lawns
and neighbours'
lawn mowers
and children
and dogs
and sprinklers
and fences

I am learning to play the piano

while every public health measure is a *lockdown*

even while my masi

with her two jobs

at the convention centre

and the nursing home

does not endure

a *lockdown*

UCP MLA Jason Stephan Unapologetic After He and MLA Pat Rehn Vacationed Out of Country over the Holidays[28]
"A Violation of Trust": Alberta Doctors Decry Government Vacations Abroad[29]

McDonald's near the Edmonton airport thrives through the travel ban
even when Diwali is cancelled, gatherings prohibited

as the Premier preaches compliance, members of his party secretly fly
to Hawai'i, Mexico

all travel is essential if you don't get caught

I get caught up in paying my rent
to the 29 percent of governing conservatives who are landlords
and to the 37 percent of official opposition who are landlords

flight delays are an inconvenience
unlike expiring Air Miles and rent left owing
equivalent emergencies
while the price of pharmacare is not

Rely on Takeout or Close Doors? A Grim Choice for Restaurants [30]

after months of hungry caution, we order takeout, support local
but by now my favourite restaurant and my favourite doctor
have permanently closed shop

I stay home so long
I keep the Alberta Motor Association in business
call them to boost my car three times in a single February

our side of Whyte Ave is concrete and dirty snow
windrows are company
stand tall without the friction of stuck tires and leaking gasoline
to melt them

Maclean's magazine calls Whyte Ave dead
and the uncontrolled leases and two-thousand-dollar one-bedrooms
aren't to blame for being full of ghosts instead of dreaming bodies

someone I used to know buys a house
worth twenty-two times my life insurance

it would take me twenty-two lifetimes
to undo the starvation my ancestors endured
that gave me this passport and diabetes,
which costs more than I
and my insurance
consent to

Reports of Domestic, Intimate Partner Violence Continue to Rise During Pandemic [31]
Calls for Alberta Tenant Protections Grow During COVID-19 Outbreak [32]
At the Corner of Loss & Renewal [33]

domestic violence goes up with the price of one-bedroom apartments
my side of the tax bracket shudders

Edmonton's previously approved Light Rail Transit
is a financial train wreck
deprioritized like safe injection sites
so that money flows into rehab, emergency rooms
instead of prevention

no one puts housing first but the research
Edmonton erects temporary shelters in convention centres
around the time that Lewis
wins his seventh Formula 1 World Championship

but no one wants to be caged in the tiny glass-walled cubicles
they call *solutions*

online netizens are mad
type *ungrateful* when they mean *worthless*

citizenry model after City Council
learn how to pass the buck without sparing any loose change
news reporters call land lines and cops to ask
why the vulnerable folks without homes are homeless

More Than 3 Million Canadians Have Diabetes, and Cases Are Growing at Alarming Rates. Do You Know the Warning Signs?[34]

I am dying
to get my diabetic test strips covered or copaid
while Formula 2 drivers risk dying
to test tracks in claustrophobic cockpits for contracts

my credit card is defrauded, cancelling my Manulife health insurance
saving me the cost of increased premiums all for the premium of self-worth
they promise to reinstate if

I have not
    fallen
    ill

or seen a doctor
received special testing
visited the emergency room
since I first bought into my own health speculation
four years ago

most diabetics diagnosed with ketoacidosis die within weeks

nothing is special
nothing is sacred
    except that which I choose to make sacred
    like what is left of my liver
    where I carry the lineage of my bapa's hunger
    in the depression between shoulder blades
    where I slotted my two memories of him

Claim Us If You're Famous [35]
Indian Americans Celebrate Vice President-Elect Kamala Harris [36]
Why Kamala Harris Matters to Me [37]

Indian women around the world
share tearful congratulations
now that Kamala Harris is Vice President of dreams

Indian women around the world
share tearful calls
voter registration
mobilizing family across borders
asking for money
and votes
for Kamala masi

now is the election that matters
and cops are Indian when it matters
this is the line that cannot be crossed

as if my best friend in Texas did not cry in the shower
the morning after her country elected Donald Trump the first time

as if everything before Kamala masi
was my best friend's fault

and every success of Kamala masi
now one for us all

I am learning to play piano
as they order Kashmiri chai
read the news

take both sides
because none of it is happening to them
until it happens to them

the American dream is enacted everywhere
and it is a nightmare for everyone, even Americans

after Lewis contracts COVID
he misses an entire Formula 1 race
returns to end the season
in a car painted with the names
of every staff member who sacrificed their health
so I could sit on my couch
and watch

by the end of 2020
Lewis wins 52 percent of all races
stands on seventeen of twenty-one podiums
and takes three grand slams

he equals the record for most World Drivers' Championships
the kids in the cars get younger each year

veteran driver Sergio Pérez wins his first race
after 190 race starts
he sprays bubbly on the top step
signs to a better team
and for a moment I cry
for the underdogs

so I work to keep my audiences and loved ones entertained
make art and write poems
visit book clubs and poetry slams
from my living room

I talk about wanting this
even as funding envelopes freeze
and things like dogs and subscriptions
become too expensive

real dogs are in high demand
puppies that grow up overwhelmed by the world
but comforted by their constant companions

cats on Zoom are the real heroes
reminding me of my humanity

National Ozempic Shortage Impacting Locals with Diabetes, Pharmacists [38]
Samsung, Ozempic and Toyota Sponsor CBC's Digital Olympic Content [39]
Why Don't "Size-Inclusive" Brands Carry Plus Sizes in Stores? [40]

pharmacies run short on melatonin and metformin
the cost of Ozempic spikes as weight crashes
celebrities siphoning hands off diabetics and addicts
will power they can afford
causing a shortage

Alberta Blue Cross is reluctant to cover it
blaming the cost of diabetes on my lazy body's "treatment resistance"
rather than Novo Nordisk or epidemiology
Novo Nordisk takes out ads at the Olympics
lining boards in ice rinks
playing between sitcoms
before horror movies
at gyms

in the media
Ozempic becomes synonymous with "cheating"
fuelling tabloid headlines like fat in fire
I throw up even water while taking it
lie on the floor or the bed for hours
waiting until side effects knock me out

my mother tells me I'm looking good
her approval is an elastic band of relativity
bound to my waist

I can't get my prescription filled
forfeit room for lemons and Diet Coke
fill drawers with vials and pens

Lululemon contracts me for a line of poetry
uses it in ads for their Winter Games
I hear my own voice boast “Canada, the brave”
directly followed by “ask your doctor about Ozempic”

I guess it works because Lululemon no longer carries my size

Canadian Mint Unveils Toonie to Mark 100th Anniversary of Insulin Discovery[41]

Frederick Banting, James Collip, and Charles Best
make history in 1921 when they sell
the first formula for insulin to Novo Nordisk for $1
haunted by the dogs who died testing it

now I buy my dad a commemorative toonie worth $2
to celebrate the bittersweet intimacy of sharing a family illness
giving in to the indulgence of buying money we can't spend

I dream of Formula 1 cars crossing lines at 350 kilometres an hour
I dream of dogs culturing acids to stop my blood glucose cresting
I dream of dogs sent to space
and dogs used as petri dishes
and dogs doing tricks for nothing close to $1

who never return

I dream of islets and vacation islands
beta cells and bureaucracy
determining how I live

science and engineering invest in my body

and on the one-hundredth anniversary of the invention of insulin
Dutch driver Max Verstappen has an eight-point lead on Lewis
in the 2021 Formula 1 World Drivers' Championship

Max is the child of a Formula 1 driver
competing for his first championship victory
Lewis is the first Black man to win
seven Formula 1 Championships
competing for a mythical eighth
in a car that can't go any faster
against a car that can't slow down

some things seem more possible
when they're at risk of being lost for good

Met Gala Organizers Face Criticism for "Gilded Glamor" Theme amid Inflation [42]
On Social Media, Activists Used the Met Gala to Call Out Stars for Gaza Silence [43]
Arise, Sir Lewis: Hamilton Knighted Three Days After F1 Title Heartbreak [44]

the revolution is forgotten
at the steps of the Met Gala
I look at photos wondering
who wore suspended disbelief and sequins
delusions and daydreams
ballgowns and bills
the best

newly knighted Sir Lewis Hamilton
        crosses
        picket
        lines

and protesters
to take his seat at the table

but these are not my problems

Why the U of A Protest Camp Raid Was a Disaster [45]
Alberta University Encampment Removals Likely Violated Protesters' Constitutional Rights, Legal Experts Say [46]
May's Auroras May Have Been Strongest for 500 Years, Says NASA [47]

these are not my people
the University of Alberta says
as they gas protesters
the same night the aurora borealis stretches
all the way to Missouri

these are not our children
the Canadian government says
as they turn away from the bombing of hospitals

these are not my legislative powers
the municipality says
they are listening
as they increase budgets for cops
tanks
traffic cams
helicopters

so how could I have asked
that my city councillors and my mayor
defend me

No Charges in Death of Ejaz Choudry, 62-Year-Old Shot and Killed by Police While in Crisis [48]
Young Woman Who Died in Halifax Walmart Oven Was Not Murdered, Police Say [49]
Watchdog Clears Toronto Police in Korchinski-Paquet Death [50]
Cargill Avoids Damages for Handling of Early Days of COVID-19 That Left Two Employees Dead, 951 with Virus [51]

my artist friends are grievers, architects of tense shoulders and creased backs
carriers of weight and weariness, infectious hope in our marrow

there are protests on the streets of Toronto
over the death of thirty-year-old Regis Korchinski-Paquet
a Black and Indigenous woman who called 9-1-1
and when officers are cleared of overt racism
I want to stop writing about it

and when Ejaz Choudry is fatally shot by police
after lighting up the mental health crisis line
I want to stop writing about it

and when nineteen-year-old Gursimran Kaur is found by her mother
in an oven of the Walmart bakery in Halifax
I want to stop writing about it

and when Cargill slaughterhouse in High River is cleared of criminal negligence
in the outbreak of 951 cases of COVID-19
and the deaths of meat shop stewards Hiep Bui and Benito Quesada
in the largest single COVID-19 outbreak in Canadian history

the tune changes
and it is Cargill Canada that is nothing like Cargill, Inc. USA
and it is Canada that's nothing like India
and Alberta that's nothing like Nova Scotia
and Edmonton that's nothing like Toronto

cops and nurses
and social workers

that are nothing like
life or death
or justice

elected men and women return home to soft beds
after another hard day's work picking who to blame
for "crisis"

citizens have no say
if they pay no property tax

my masi pays for calling cards instead of land lines
and the government takes her money for land mines

my mami is busy waiting for the price of gas to fall
leaves early to bypass white supremacist anti-vax parades to get to the hospital
on time

I try to believe that the blame is a slow roast
that falls off with patience
that the bones remaining
offer sustenance
when all I feel is hunger

I try to believe
that if I know enough truth
they cannot bury me in a lie

I am out of my twenties
they don't make thirty-dollar bills
I am out of fives
I don't know anything about coinage and laundering
I'm out of change
even for the washing machine

I invested my youth in politick
spent hot weeks door knocking and speech writing
the decade that the Province broke forty years straight of conservative
leadership

I invested in hope
and watched its worth plummet
as my politicians broke every promise
pulling off their faces to reveal the same faces
I had seen my whole life

and now I understand it is my anger
not my love
that makes me a poet

Alberta Restaurant Owners Frustrated as COVID-19 Closures Cut Into Prime Patio Season [52]
Migrant Workers at Red Deer Slaughterhouse Say They've Felt Unfair Blame amid Growing COVID-19 Outbreak [53]
A UN Report Slammed the Predatory Practices of Canada's TFW Program. Some of the Worst Abuses of This "Breeding Ground" for Modern Slavery Are Here in Alberta [54]

people are dying of COVID
old people, whose bodies are done with laughter
sick people, whose lives are done with their bodies

it is a lockdown

MEAT off Whyte Ave puts out more patio heaters
the big businesses take out COVID loans
my dad's auto-body shop runs on unpaid labour and gasoline poisoning
hardens his skin

Yoshi's Sushi is too authentic to stay afloat
beneath the vegan bar
people wait in line outside to go dancing
throw plastic shells of vape pens in the gutter before ordering
plant-based fried chicken

I walk to the grocer for chicken and garlic
Edmontonians on the internet talk about dead Whyte Ave
blame a lack of ingenuity and skill

my face looks more and more like the scapegoat
they keep offering me for dinner

in 2021
curfew is ten o'clock

which means happy hour still ends at eight
and when me and my fiancé run to the old Mac's

we hold our breath so that we don't fog up our glasses
around the bar crowd buying lottery tickets

across the street, The King and I shuts down
leaving me with memories of eating Thai food alone
even on the dates I wasn't alone

on the walk home I count
three sour cola gummies
and how much fast-acting insulin I will inject
to enjoy them

surely things will get better

because hope has become a scarce commodity
a federal bond with low interest
and as usual, it is the minorities
with the thick skin on their backs
who run out first

in 2022, my Mac's becomes a Circle K
my boyfriend becomes my fiancé
The King and I becomes an Indian restaurant
I use more insulin now
and the taste of Coke Zero stays the same

I wonder if the Indian clerk knows
I am glad to see him so far from home
the tap-to-pay a handshake between people
who didn't know they needed it

I smile at him beneath my mask
he asks if four bottles of kombucha are everything
I can't carry more than this moment
my pancreas has too few beta cells to process
the sweetness I really crave

Casinos and Bingo Halls Readying to Reopen as Alberta Government Forecasts Rebound in Gaming Revenue [55]
Alberta Passes iGaming Act: Major Expansion of Online Gambling Industry [56]

while the casinos are closed in 2020
Alberta non-profits reliant on government funding
go under, scale back, drown in the green rooms
of shows cancelled
without pay

I leave my job as a festival director
after cutting my own salary twice
wonder if getting grants is a form of blood money
when the Alberta government raises those funds
from gamblers goaded into good times

and soon it is out of my hands
like money leaving gamblers' palms

when the government lifts restrictions
casinos are booming

I feel sick writing about it

4,289 words

India Coronavirus: The Man Giving Dignified Burial to COVID-19 Victims[57]
Deaths Climb as India Reels from Deadly COVID Wave[58]

funeral homes are backed up
and memorials go unattended

in Surat, Gujarat
families take shifts at funerals
while the crematoriums melt from overuse

NHL Faces Backlash over Report League Wants to Buy COVID-19 Vaccines for Players [59]
Canada Can't Stop Corporations from Buying Coronavirus Vaccines: Hajdu [60]
"It Isn't a Hoax": Alberta Family Grieves as Father Lies Dying of COVID-19 in B.C. Hospital [61]

every day I wonder if I'm imagining things

as grieving sons and daughters share screenshots
of their final moments with parents, friends
as baas and dadas line up for a vaccine
promised to athletes and managers of the National Hockey League

the City does its part:
cashiers at brand-name grocers charge twenty-five cents for bags
electronic scooters are licensed for anyone with a credit card
but bike lanes don't get wider
a man is struck and killed on my street
and neither Lime nor Bird are penalized

a man dies in my masi's nursing home
with only my masi to eulogize him

Whyte Ave is dead
so a new Winners opens over the body
of a bookstore
bars go up in the windows at night
security at attention
even in minus thirty degrees

every week I call my father and my doctor

sometimes their concern is a clamp
holding the pieces of my body together

"Living in a Tin Can": Edmonton Doctor on Out-of-This-World Mission in Utah [62]
Mars Rover Landing: Nasa's Perseverance Touches Down Safely in Search of Life [63]

my friend Shawna is training to be an astronaut

she lives underwater
floats in zero gravity
talks at length about Mars
and for a second, I daydream of an emptiness
that confirms possibility

in space-time's continual quest for meaning
the Mars rover Perseverance touches down successfully

I cry, thinking that there must be children
who worked quietly their whole lives for this
they cheer in a NASA control room

Edmonton Council Approves Zero Tax Increase Next Year [64]
Fun Things to Do in Edmonton Area During COVID-19 Alberta Reopening Phase [65]
Edmonton's Mandatory Mask Bylaw to End on July 1 After City Council Vote [66]

Edmonton does not raise taxes in crisis
but I lie awake, wondering
which part of the Municipal Government Act, Section 7
is preventing them from spending on shelters and housing and transit
in the name of safety, health, and welfare?

but I only spent ten years studying politics
so what would an insurance risk like me
know about it

my fiancé was once a marine biologist
shows me emails where aquarists ask each other things like
"does anyone want two mated sharks or seventy-two jellyfish?"

my fiancé and I don't need sharks
but we are invited to the Vancouver Aquarium
introduced to the smell of otters
thick and cloudy fishiness in my nose
sun-baked saltiness
glass that quakes
and quarantined animals
too sick or angry
for the public to see

backstage, the aquarium wears the dust of a dressing room
corner dregs and unready things

we see mostly

sinks   drains   pipes   glass   buckets

salt and water

we see a tank with sea sponges
creatures so ancient in their origin
that we lack the knowledge to know if these ones
are even still alive

and down a dead end
we come to a black box sealed with a damp lid
and a heavy padlock
a cage weighed down with crates

a thick window of glass lets us catch a flash of moving red
she is *swimming*

the guy making minimum wage
becomes a sea keeper,
unclasping and

lifting, lifting

until the smooth suctioning arm of a giant Pacific octopus hooks around
his fingers

and he laughs, says

"she's quite gentle"

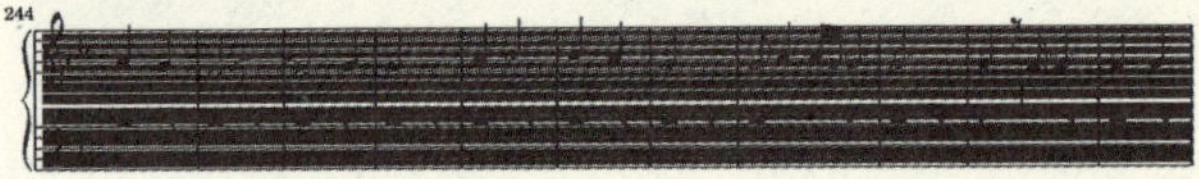

my fiancé's hand is a ladder
she grips his palm in a handshake
then falls away

an octopus can fit into the smallest of openings
body squeezed in a collapse that would kill animals like me

[redacted]

she's a beast

and my mercy is that I am one too
but only on dry land

Edmonton Election 2021: Amarjeet Sohi Elected Mayor [67]
Alberta Election 2023: UCP Wins Majority Government, but Loses Key Seats [68]
Meet the Mayoral Candidates Running in Edmonton's 2025 Municipal Election [69]
Recap: Liberals Hold Edmonton Centre, Conservatives Pick Up Griesbach, Rural Sweep for Tories [70]

it's an election year

candidates kiss boots
wipe mud off their lips
behind closed doors

sometimes my masi asks me to write eulogies
for her patients at the nursing home

she says
"no one's there but me"

and I hear

"I am the last one to have given love"

her sense of duty is embedded, scar tissue now soft
her work is the work of necessity
and she does it because it needs doing

I gather her notes on his smile
his belligerence with the nurses
how he tried chaos on everyone but her
ask questions
                about food and laughter
                breaths exhaled in the company of others
before composing in words
what her tongue tangles to translate from her heart

Lewis loses the 2021 Formula 1 World Drivers' Championship
on another day of death and disease in Alberta

Lewis loses the 2022 Formula 1 World Drivers' Championship

Lewis loses the 2023 Formula 1 World Drivers' Championship

Lewis loses the 2024 Formula 1 World Drivers' Championship

Lewis loses the 2025 Formula 1 World Drivers' Championship
on another day of death and disease in Alberta

diabetes has abandoned my taste
for mango lassi
masala cha
and jalebi

time has abandoned my faith
in celebration
in sweetness
in new beginnings

my friend
and my masis
and my cousins
and my sister

all return to work
for the 120th week or the 27th month or the second-and-a-half year in a row
staffing their way through protests at hospital doors
they tune out the news in break rooms
while they text pictures of flames, lamps, burning wicks of ghee
it is Diwali again

they ask
"have you eaten?"

I can't remember Diwali or New Year's
        whether it is snowing or cold
        if I turned off the stove
        or left the lights on

Why Are Wildfires So Common Now?[71]
A History of Cuts to Alberta's Firefighting Budget, Explained[72]
Much of Alberta, Saskatchewan Under a Blanket of Wildfire Smoke, Air Quality Warnings[73]

in the endless summers of the endless pandemics
the Province goes up in flames

British Columbia and Alberta take turns blowing the blame away
the Conservatives try to save money
gutting the jobs of emergency firefighters to win votes
as if ecological disaster is a bet and not an insurance scam

my asthma does somersaults my body cannot handle
takes up residence in my esophagus like a *Ghostbusters* villain
my lungs use my body
say my words
dictate my plans

my eczema explodes
like a tree touched by lightning or hoarfrost
I stay on the floor another summer
weaving my own lockdown into public health measures
that don't exist anymore

I am in too much pain to pray

my hands bed the seeds of small blisters
the size of pincushion heads
summer flings
the inflammation grows in tiny white bumps
along every part of palm
they fill with clear fluid
not blood or pus
burst when I pinch

I am aware each time like it's the first
that the largest organ in the human body
is skin

my masi is always the first
to hear when I have a big gig at the Shaw Conference Centre

her uniform is black and white
shoes glued with cushioned soles
embossed name tag no one needs
when they are around her

a few years ago
she worked the hardest wedding of her life
eight hundred people
fifty showing up without RSVPS
asking for doubles without tips

I don't think I'll ever feel at home onstage
when I know how heavy the servers' jugs are
how meticulously each sprig of broccolini has been plated

I don't think of my cousins, my masi,
and my other relatives
as having an *in*
that actually gets us out of this
she tells me she always says
"yup, that's my Nisha"

I perform until two days before *lockdown*
drive from back-to-back gigs over icy streets
on the March road between Calgary and Edmonton

she worked until she was mandated not to
a gig worker in the entertainment business like me

I am learning to write music

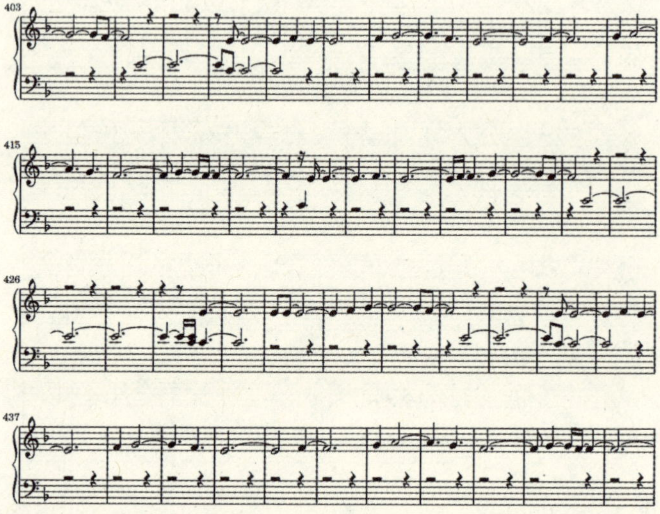
403
415
426
437
448
459

470
481
492
504
515
526

312
318
401
407

the gig economy collapses

and suddenly it's not just people that are dying, but the arts
and in emergency meetings
governments decide that one-time grants will save us
an injection of money
administered like an EpiPen

I can't tell funders that we were doomed
even before lockdowns

four mid-size venues in a city of one million shut down
before January of 2020
my credit plummets
because the festival I love
can't pay me
and all I hear is the same old line
that back in the day
we did it because it made us happy

More Than 700 Trees at Risk in Edmonton's Hawrelak Park Renewal: Report[74]

no one with the money wants to keep the arts alive
unless it makes them money
no one with the money wants to keep the trees alive
unless it makes them money
no one with the money wants to keep the money alive
if it costs them money

they want a poet laureate to lift spirits, celebrate our city
absolve them of the whispering regrets buzzing in their baby hairs
as they send men to sand stumps at the place where
100-year-old trees are cut

the trees in Hawrelak Park are thick like my father's knuckles
they are connected and held together like flexing bones
recombinant to the sluggish skin of my burning neck
when I recall all the memories of all Heritage Days Festivals
spent here

branches tangle with each other
they are known to each other

this is the best spot for eating mangoes on the August long weekend
folks with sunscreen wait in hot lines for Indian food
and no one over the age of forty in my family believes in waiting
or sun protection

on her day off, my masi
rides the bus from the Meadows Transit Centre to Hawrelak
tastes, listens
the line for camel is long
she shows her son a world she knew first
but not better

smoke and scent transport her closer to home
the ginger beer here is fresher
the mangoes come with chili
she is fluent in five languages

she spills a little water to feed the ground
quench it like her inflamed tendons too are quenched
in the cool dirt that seems a miracle in the heat of the stripped valley

the roots hold
the way the house in Millwoods
always held everyone who came

this is the loyalty of bark
I believe in good times
in the water

in what becomes of us when we're gone
and what becomes a part of us when we're here

Patio Permit Fees, Cuts to Arts and Sports Groups on List as Edmonton Looks to Trim Budget[75]
How Much Would You Pay for the Arts?[76]
Letters Sept. 11: Stop Coddling Alberta's Anti-Vaxxers[77]

there is no fruit to ripen in the trees
left to bake in the concrete of Churchill Square
but the canopies of relief are sweet

one tree over there plays mother
this one a bike rack
that one the clothesline

the City asks me not to write about politics
so I pace Churchill Square and try to write its eulogy

I felt the City sweep me under the rug of 2020
denying the violence in my direct messages of racists calling me ungrateful
anti-vaxxers commenting on Instagram about COVID being a hoax
and the anonymous hate mail that came my way

but the streets are cleaned when it snows
even as the arts budget freezes
and neither my city councillors nor my mayor protect me

so I tell the truth I know:
that the City I love does not always love me

and when others ask me how I was given such an honour
I say I applied, interviewed well, did not beg
because that's what business school taught me

I am wrong for thinking it meant something to succeed
and wanting it so bad while others suffered
to blame audiences for not attending
or venues for overcharging
or festivals for underpaying

I was wrong for cashing the cheques
I was wrong for thinking success was hard work done alone
and that I was smart and clever
that they found other bodies to bury first

like my masa
whose eulogy I wrote for my mother through a text message

like my father's best friend
who spoke so little English but still laughed when I did

like the first worker to die from COVID in Alberta
a woman with a pocket full of candy
packing meat at Cargill
where only the managers got the masks

I feel sick of writing
I feel sick about it

as a child
I'd go all sorts of places with my dad
Totem, Home Depot
End of the Roll carpets
Big Al's fish store where we watched sharks being fed

when I visit my dad
I count the fish in his tanks
I dream underwater
until I remember

I think about my fighting fish, freshwater long gone
his body now soil under a tree

I learned grief first through goldfish
then angelfish, cichlids
and algae-eating suckerfish

it's been nearly two decades since my betta died
now, I make poetry of his body

on the day Max Verstappen
is handed the 2021 Formula 1 World Drivers' Championship trophy
I add words to a poem like a death knell

Max wins again, and again, and again

numbers rise
trophies and words and bodies
climb like championship points
nothing real until it has been timed, measured, counted
despite fewer deaths from COVID
being timed, measured, and counted

but slowing down
in the face of a 350 kilometres per hour pandemic is unfathomable

and the City tells me
if I die of COVID like I thought I might
hunched on the floor with a pulse oximeter and a vaporizer
they can simply change the line on year-end financial statements
to read "respiratory complications"
rather than "Delta" or "Omicron"

and the Province tells me
that they no longer need to report acute care outbreaks
or total COVID deaths
beyond the last five years
so by the time you read this
thousands more will be off the record

they're busy in their grief
over how small their pay raises were
how they had to cull half the proposed increase in police budgets
how their kids and grandkids and constituents all want to go no-contact
when they've done nothing wrong

I think about Christmas
I think about Easter, about rebirth

I think about grocery prices
clawbacks on COVID relief
austerity tightening a fist around my heart
inflation making a crisis of my dreams

I think about what to cook, again
while beaten wives hungry for change
are confined at home
in lockdown's grip

I think about home

and mostly I think about death

how my faith in politics died first in a refrigerator truck
then a field hospital

how tracking the speed at which we can free up ICU beds
is a success story and not a tragedy

and when tiki-torchbearers think it's their God-given right to sentence the rest of the world to death

I wonder
what God they will face
and how much I will pay
in my people's blood
to see it?

Airline Required to Compensate Families of Flight PS752 Victims, Ontario Court Rules[78]
The World Has Moved On. But Those Who Lost Loved Ones to COVID-19 Feel Stuck in Time[79]
Alberta COVID Babies Are Now Off to Kindergarten[80]

I write letters to Dr. Li Wenliang

first in the chords of my arteries
then my veins
then the musical chambers
of my heart

I write them in blood
and guilt
and grief

I write them in anger

I memorize his name
his face
his sentencing

I memorize the way the Government of China
posthumously calls him a "martyr"
for sounding the alert on COVID
when no one else wanted to believe him

as if he chose to be a martyr and not a doctor
a man who did not let his fear
consume him

I can't hold the bodies in this poem
no memorial for the dying
when they are still dying
being erased as I type
no flowers on stones for the hospitals
no retribution for people
who died in hallways
under fluorescent lights
because there just wasn't enough profit
in saving them

I am a masi now
and my nephew is a recentring
a type of gravity I cannot name
a force as invisible as an exhale
as natural as a deep breath

and I wonder if we will see the end of this
before my friend makes it to the Moon or Mars
or NASA sends dreamers into the stars
with missions named for metaphors

I wonder if the children piecing these stories together
will ask if I was angry
if the numbers made me cry or shake
if I would have done things differently

because sometimes I get onstage and think of my two-year-old nephew
born in the cloudy waters of an atmospheric river in Oregon
the gentle sway of his mother's love
that defies my understanding of fullness

and I feel guilty and joyful
                    and furious and hopeful
                    about the world we made him
                    all at once

COVID-19 Is Six Today. What We've Learned[81]

once in 2020
I watched six-time Formula 1
World Drivers' Champion Lewis Hamilton
win a race on only three wheels

        it was summer at Silverstone
        his left front tire blew out on the last lap
        and his thirty-second lead disappeared
        at 350 kilometres an hour
        with Max Verstappen in his mirrors

                the press of hot air and gravity
                rubber treads rubbing asphalt
                a checkered flag waving
                a car and a body
                the sun through the halo
                shining in his eyes

and now I understand it is my love
and not my anger
that makes me a poet

soon,
like a Whyte Ave summer
we will tremble and sweat in the heat
of a time so good we know it
while we're in it

we will know the taste of time
sweetened by the sun
when we hold these names near teeth and tongue

the patios will be busy
the wasps will be dormant
        feasted as they are on mosquitoes
        and other pests

and I'll get a call
        from my city
        or my masi
        or my nephew

asking me
to write about it

ACKNOWLEDGMENTS

I owe an unpayable debt to 7,113 people who died from COVID-19 in Alberta as of January 2026, when the last count was made for this book. This poem was first 432 words (432 trackable deaths from COVID). It grew to version 615 (when it was first performed live), 719, and 1,827. Counting becomes less precise through both government obfuscation and antiscience rhetoric. Numbers get blurry but I've done the best I can, with help from the University of Alberta's Open Publishing & Government Information Librarian, Katie Cuyler, who helped me track down early data that had been removed from the Government of Alberta websites.

I served as the Poet Laureate for the City of Edmonton from 2019 to 2021. Edmonton believes in poetry. They invest in it, they inspire it, they house it and feed it and let it grow. They treat Poet Laureateships as investments in community, not accolades or honours at the end of a career. No city is perfect. But Edmonton is my home, and my success is rooted here and was nurtured by the City's support for the arts.

This work was funded in part by Canada's Social Sciences and Humanities Research Council (SSHRC) and the UBC School of Creative Writing. Nalo Hopkinson was especially thoughtful and kind in navigating the dehumanizing feeling of applying for funding and was a large part of advocating for me and my wonky transcripts.

My MFA supervisor, Cecily Nicholson, treated the work with respect and care while still guiding me to make it rhetorically and academically more robust. We added things like line breaks and a table of contents, but she also pushed me to write a book as if it was for a community who shares my politics, not just opposes them. I'm an angry person but the people I'm mad at don't read my work! Cecily was right, and she turned this from a book of hurt and anger to a book of homage and love.

Omar El Akkad, my faculty at the Banff Centre residency, read it and pushed me to consider the urgency of the work. When I asked if people really wanted to read about COVID-19 as it was still happening, Omar not only said they would, but that they needed to. Faith in your writing is a powerful gift to be given.

Arsenal Pulp has been an incredible leader in disability literature, and they have continued to queer and dismantle the academy through supporting marginalized voices. I am in such good company with them, and I am grateful for their support through every challenge and difficulty I've had with this work (including pushing every deadline they made for me, sorry).

My editor, Katherine Abbass, is a close friend but also the dream critique partner. She is the only one I trust to know exactly where I can push my work while keeping my voice and story intact. She is one of a kind: a gifted editor as well as a gifted writer.

The many folks who have inspired my work: Jasbir K. Puar, Mercedes Eng, Jordan Scott, Moez Surani, Claudia Rankine, Jordan Abel, JJJJJerome Ellis, Jane Shi, Leah Lakshmi Piepzna-Samarasinha, Hanif Abdurraqib, Travis Chi Wing Lau, Dr. Scott Knowles and the *COVIDcalls* podcast, the *COVID Collections* project in Edmonton, Rebecca Salazar, Dr. Li Wenliang, Hiep Bui, Jes Battis, Conyer Clayton, Tea Gerbeza, Shane Neilson, Cassandra Myers, Kay Kassirer, Medgine Mathurin, Titilope Sonuga, Simina Banu, my masis, and my nephews.

And lastly, to my husband and academic ally (and writer himself), Matthew James Weigel, who has read every word of every poem I have ever written for almost a decade now. Maybe you're not supposed to date a writer when you're a writer, but think of it as a way to get cheap editing and it isn't so bad.

NOTES

1 Alex Antoneshyn, "This Poem Is Alive. 615 Albertans Who Had COVID-19 Are Not. As More Die, the Poem Will Grow," *CTV News*, December 7, 2020, https://www.ctvnews.ca/edmonton/article/this-poem-is-alive-615-albertans-who-had-covid-19-are-not-as-more-die-the-poem-will-grow/.

2 "'I Am So, So Sad': Husband, Friends of Cargill Worker Who Died from COVID-19 Honour Her in Memorial," *CBC News*, May 4, 2020, https://www.cbc.ca/news/canada/calgary/memorial-worker-cargill-hiep-bui-covid-death-alberta-1.5554765.

3 Jeff Slack, "High River Cargill Workers Being Neglected PPE Equipment amid COVID-19 Outbreak," *CityNews*, April 18, 2020, https://calgary.citynews.ca/2020/04/18/high-river-cargill-workers-being-neglected-ppe-equipment-amid-covid-19-outbreak/.

4 "Canada's Victims of Flight PS752," *CBC News*, January 10, 2020, https://www.cbc.ca/news2/interactives/flightps752/.

5 "Hamilton Seals Historic 7th Title with Peerless Wet-Weather Victory in Turkey," Formula 1, November 15, 2020, https://www.formula1.com/en/latest/article/hamilton-seals-historic-7th-title-with-peerless-wet-weather-victory-in.4wK1atemiXDvWXQxOknL4J.

6 Emily Rae Pasiuk, "COVID-19 Restrictions Putting Out the Light of Diwali in Edmonton," *CBC News*, November 13, 2020, https://www.cbc.ca/news/canada/edmonton/diwali-covid-19-restrictions-edmonton-1.5801164.

7 Michael Brown, "How COVID-19 Overwhelmed Canada's Long-Term Care System," *Folio*, April 22, 2020, https://www.ualberta.ca/en/folio/2020/04/how-covid-19-overwhelmed-canadas-long-term-care-system.html.

8 Lauren Boothby, "COVID-19: Nurses May Be Recalled as ICUs, ERs in Edmonton and South Zone Under Pressure, Alberta's Hospitalizations Pass 200," *Edmonton Journal*, August 20, 2021, https://edmontonjournal.com/news/local-news/covid-19-nurses-to-be-recalled-as-icu-ers-in-edmonton-and-south-zone-under-pressure-albertas-hospitalizations-pass-200.

9 Heide Pearson, "COVID-19: Staff at Calgary Hospitals Told to 'Engage in Oxygen Conservation' as Cases Rise," *Global News*, November 30, 2020, https://globalnews.ca/news/7492963/coronavirus-calgary-hospitals-oxygen-conservation/.

10 "How Alberta's COVID-19 Crisis Became 'Absolutely Frightening,'" *Maclean's*, May 4, 2021, https://macleans.ca/news/canada/covid-19-how-albertas-crisis-became-absolutely-frightening/.

11 Susan Krashinsky Robertson, "Aritzia Weathers the COVID-19 Storm with Increase in E-Commerce Sales," *The Globe and Mail*, June 7, 2020, https://www.theglobeandmail.com/business/article-aritzia-weathers-the-covid-19-storm-with-increase-in-e-commerce-sales/.

12 Violet Moya, "Opinion: Sephora Never Valued Workers Like Me," *The New York Times*, April 18, 2020, https://www.nytimes.com/2020/04/18/opinion/sephora-layoffs-coronavirus.html.

13 Chris Baraniuk, "No End to COVID-19 Webcam Shortage," *BBC News*, July 25, 2020, https://www.bbc.com/news/technology-53506401.

14 "F1 Confirm 2020 Azerbaijan, Singapore and Japanese Grands Prix Have Been Cancelled," Formula 1, accessed March 2, 2026, https://www.formula1.com/en/latest/article/f1-confirm-2020-azerbaijan-singapore-and-japanese-grands-prix-have-been.53mR0P305L9eUmDJXYOFoh.

15 "5 Steps F1 Is Taking to Ensure Racing Is as Safe as Possible When the 2020 Season Starts," Formula 1, accessed March 2, 2026, https://www.formula1.com/en/latest/article/5-steps-f1-is-taking-to-ensure-racing-is-as-safe-as-possible-when-the-2020.2Hmwu17Z4SDTMDGboZ2Iac.

16 Keith Collantine, "F1 Will Not Cancel Races If a Driver Tests Positive for COVID-19," *RaceFans*, June 2, 2020, https://www.racefans.net/2020/06/02/f1-will-not-cancel-races-if-a-driver-tests-positive-for-covid-19/.

17 Giles Richards, "Romain Grosjean's 'Life Saved' by Halo After Remarkable Escape at Bahrain GP," *The Guardian*, November 29, 2020, https://www.theguardian.com/sport/2020/nov/29/romain-grosjean-f1-crash-bahrain-gp.

18 Stephanie Babych, "Calgary Police and Anti-Mask Protesters Clash at Weekend Protests; Alberta Surpasses 90,000 COVID-19 Cases," *Calgary Herald*, December 20, 2020, https://calgaryherald.com/news/local-news/calgary-police-and-anti-mask-protesters-clash-at-weekend-protests-alberta-surpasses-90000-covid-19-cases.

19 Laurence Edmondson, "How 2020 Changed Lewis Hamilton," ESPN, December 23, 2020, https://www.espn.com/f1/story/_/id/30587297/how-2020-changed-lewis-hamilton.

20 "Evidence Suggests SARS-CoV-2 Spike Protein Can Enter the Brain," *Clinical OMICs* 8, no. 1: 13 (2021), https://doi.org/10.1089/clinomi.08.01.17.

21 Dave Mitchell, "'The Whole World Is My Karaoke Machine': Singing Mailman Brings Smiles to Edmonton Streets," *CTV News*, December 5, 2019, https://www.ctvnews.ca/edmonton/article/the-whole-world-is-my-karaoke-machine-singing-mailman-brings-smiles-to-edmonton-streets/.

22 Sean Amato, "Kenney Quiet on Protesters After Issuing COVID-19 'Wake Up Call' to South Asian Community," *CTV News*, November 29, 2020, https://www.ctvnews.ca/edmonton/article/kenney-quiet-on-protesters-after-issuing-covid-19-wake-up-call-to-south-asian-community/.

23 Rishi Nagar, "Opinion: Stop Stigmatizing South Asians for High Infection Rates," *CBC News*, December 8, 2020, https://www.cbc.ca/news/canada/calgary/road-ahead-calgary-south-asian-covid-stigma-1.5831196.

24 Sammy Hudes, "Kenney's 'Wake-Up Call' to Northeast Calgary Condemned as 'Scapegoating,'" *Calgary Herald*, November 30, 2020, https://calgaryherald.com/news/politics/kenneys-wake-up-call-to-northeast-calgary-condemned-as-scapegoating.

25 Blake Lough, "From Books to Beer, COVID-19 Sparks Delivery Boom in Alberta," *Global News*, March 20, 2020, https://globalnews.ca/news/6711555/coronavirus-covid-19-alberta-books-beer-groceries-delivery/.

26 Today's Trucking, "Alberta Takes Steps to Ease Regulatory Burden on Truck Drivers During COVID-19 Response," trucknews.com, April 10, 2020, https://www.trucknews.com/regulations/alberta-takes-steps-to-ease-regulatory-burden-on-truck-drivers-during-covid-19-response/1003139393/.

27 "How Delivery Drivers Became Vital in the Pandemic," *BBC News*, December 24, 2020, video, 1 min., 26 sec., https://www.bbc.com/news/world-us-canada-55441645.

28 Lisa Johnson, "UCP MLA Jason Stephan Unapologetic After He and MLA Pat Rehn Vacationed Out of Country over the Holidays," *Edmonton Journal*, January 3, 2021, https://edmontonjournal.com/news/politics/following-up-on-govt-staff-mlas-travelling-outside-of-canada.

29 Jason Herring, "'A Violation of Trust': Alberta Doctors Decry Government Vacations Abroad," *Calgary Herald*, January 2, 2021, https://calgaryherald.com/news/politics/a-violation-of-trust-alberta-doctors-decry-government-vacations-abroad.

30 Daniel Austin, "Rely on Takeout or Close Doors? A Grim Choice for Restaurants," *Calgary Herald*, March 20, 2020, https://calgaryherald.com/business/local-business/rely-on-takeout-or-close-doors-a-grim-choice-for-restaurants.

31 Nicole Thompson, "Reports of Domestic, Intimate Partner Violence Continue to Rise During Pandemic," *CBC News*, February 15, 2021, https://www.cbc.ca/news/canada/toronto/domestic-intimate-partner-violence-up-in-pandemic-1.5914344.

32 Jordan Omstead, "Calls for Alberta Tenant Protections Grow During COVID-19 Outbreak," *CBC News*, March 24, 2020, https://www.cbc.ca/news/canada/edmonton/alberta-tenant-protections-covid-1.5509020.

33 Jason Markusoff, "At the Corner of Loss & Renewal," *Maclean's*, November 2020, 56–59.

34 Karen Hawthorne, "More Than 3 Million Canadians Have Diabetes, and Cases Are Growing at Alarming Rates. Do You Know the Warning Signs?," Healthing.ca, November 12, 2021, https://www.healthing.ca/diabetes/diabetes-symptoms-info.

35 Kumari Devarajan, "Claim Us If You're Famous," NPR, November 10, 2020, https://www.npr.org/2020/11/10/933631207/claim-us-if-youre-famous.

36 Lauren Frayer, "Indian Americans Celebrate Vice President-Elect Kamala Harris," NPR, November 8, 2020, https://www.npr.org/sections/live-updates-2020-election-results/2020/11/08/932824125/indian-americans-rejoice-as-kamala-harris-prepares-to-become-the-next-vice-presi.

37 Manisha Sinha, "Why Kamala Harris Matters to Me," *The New York Times*, August 12, 2020, https://www.nytimes.com/2020/08/12/opinion/kamala-harris-indian-american.html.

38 Jennifer Dorozio, "National Ozempic Shortage Impacting Locals with Diabetes, Pharmacists," *CBC News*, October 7, 2023, https://www.cbc.ca/news/canada/calgary/ozempic-shortage-calgary-1.6989883.

39 Nick Krewen, "Samsung, Ozempic and Toyota Sponsor CBC's Digital Olympic Content," *Media in Canada*, February 7, 2022, https://mediaincanada.com/2022/02/07/samsung-ozempic-and-toyota-sponsor-cbcs-digital-olympic-content/.

40 Gianluca Russo, "Why Don't 'Size-Inclusive' Brands Carry Plus Sizes in Stores?," *Refinery 29*, March 23, 2022, https://www.refinery29.com/en-us/2022/03/10874398/plus-size-in-store-shopping-brands.

41 Denise Wong and Mike Lloyd, "Canadian Mint Unveils Toonie to Mark 100th Anniversary of Insulin Discovery," *CityNews*, July 13, 2021, https://vancouver.citynews.ca/2021/07/13/toonie-insulin-royal-canadian-mint/.

42 Maya Yang, "Met Gala Organizers Face Criticism for 'Gilded Glamor' Theme amid Inflation," *The Guardian*, May 2, 2022, https://www.theguardian.com/fashion/2022/may/02/met-gala-theme-gilded-glamor-criticism-inflation.

43 Chloe Veltman, "On Social Media, Activists Used the Met Gala to Call Out Stars for Gaza Silence," NPR, May 11, 2024, https://www.npr.org/2024/05/11/1250506915/met-gala-block-israel.

44 PA Media, "Arise, Sir Lewis: Hamilton Knighted Three Days After F1 Title Heartbreak," *The Guardian*, December 15, 2021, https://www.theguardian.com/sport/2021/dec/15/arise-sir-lewis-hamilton-knighted-three-days-after-f1-title-heartbreak.

45 David Climenhaga, "Why the U of A Protest Camp Raid Was a Disaster," *The Tyee*, May 17, 2024, https://thetyee.ca/Opinion/2024/05/17/University-of-Alberta-Protest-Camp-Raid-Disaster/.

46 Matt Scace, "Alberta University Encampment Removals Likely Violated Protesters' Constitutional Rights, Legal Experts Say," *Calgary Herald*, May 11, 2024, https://calgaryherald.com/news/local-news/alberta-university-encampment-removals-likely-violated-protesters-constitutional-rights-legal-experts-say.

47 Jamie Carter, "May's Auroras May Have Been Strongest for 500 Years, Says NASA," *Forbes*, May 22, 2024, https://www.forbes.com/sites/jamiecartereurope/2024/05/22/mays-auroras-may-have-been-strongest-for-500-years-says-nasa/.

48 Shanifa Nasser, "No Charges in Death of Ejaz Choudry, 62-Year-Old Shot and Killed by Police While in Crisis," *CBC News*, April 6, 2021, https://www.cbc.ca/news/canada/toronto/ejaz-choudry-no-charges-siu-peel-police-1.5976266.

49 Chris Lambie, "Young Woman Who Died in Halifax Walmart Oven Was Not Murdered, Police Say," *National Post*, November 18, 2024, https://nationalpost.com/news/canada/halifax-walmart-oven-death-not-suspicious.

50 "Watchdog Clears Toronto Police in Korchinski-Paquet Death," *BBC News*, August 26, 2020, https://www.bbc.com/news/world-us-canada-53923362.

51 Matt Scace, "Cargill Avoids Damages for Handling of Early Days of COVID-19 That Left Two Employees Dead, 951 with Virus," *Calgary Herald*, June 19, 2024, https://calgaryherald.com/business/local-business/cargill-avoids-damages-early-days-covid-19.

52 "Alberta Restaurant Owners Frustrated as COVID-19 Closures Cut Into Prime Patio Season," *CBC News*, May 5, 2021, https://www.cbc.ca/news/canada/calgary/alberta-restaurant-closures-1.6015599.

53 Joel Dryden and Sarah Rieger, "Migrant Workers at Red Deer Slaughterhouse Say They've Felt Unfair Blame amid Growing COVID-19 Outbreak," *CBC News*, February 22, 2021, https://www.cbc.ca/news/canada/calgary/olymel-workers-1.5922392.

54 Jeremy Appel, "A UN Report Slammed the Predatory Practices of Canada's TFW Program. Some of the Worst Abuses of This 'Breeding Ground' for Modern Slavery Are Here in Alberta," *Progress Report*, October 12, 2023, https://www.theprogressreport.ca/a_recent_report_from_the_un_slammed_the_predatory_practices_of_canada_s_tfw_program_some_of_the_worst_abuses_are_here_in_alberta.

55 Lisa Johnson, "Casinos and Bingo Halls Readying to Reopen as Alberta Government Forecasts Rebound in Gaming Revenue," *Edmonton Journal*, March 7, 2021, https://edmontonjournal.com/news/politics/budget-follow-government-gambling-on-rebound-in-gaming-revenue.

56 Daniel Hunter, "Alberta Passes iGaming Act: Major Expansion of Online Gambling Industry," *Casino Industry News*, May 9, 2025, https://casinoindustrynews.com/gambling-news/alberta-passes-igaming-act-major-expansion-of-online-gambling-industry/.

57 "India Coronavirus: The Man Giving Dignified Burial to COVID-19 Victims," *BBC News*, April 28, 2020, https://www.bbc.com/news/world-asia-india-52380573.

58 "Deaths Climb as India Reels from Deadly COVID Wave," *BBC News*, April 24, 2021, https://www.bbc.com/news/world-asia-india-56855712.

59 Hana Mae Nassar, "NHL Faces Backlash over Report League Wants to Buy COVID-19 Vaccines for Players," *City News*, December 11, 2020, https://edmonton.citynews.ca/2020/12/11/nhl-backlash-covid-19-vaccines/.

60 Rachael D'Amore, "Canada Can't Stop Corporations from Buying Coronavirus Vaccines: Hajdu," *Global News*, December 11, 2020, https://globalnews.ca/news/7516433/coronavirus-vaccine-nhl-buying/.

61 Sarah Ryan, "'It Isn't a Hoax': Alberta Family Grieves as Father Lies Dying of COVID-19 in B.C. Hospital," *Global News*, November 20, 2020, https://globalnews.ca/news/7476258/alberta-man-dying-coronavirus-covid/.

62 Wallis Snowdon, "'Living in a Tin Can': Edmonton Doctor on Out-of-This-World Mission in Utah," *CBC News*, January 20, 2020, https://www.cbc.ca/news/canada/edmonton/edmonton-space-astronaut-mars-mission-shawna-pandya-1.5433027.

63 Natalie Grover, "Mars Rover Landing: Nasa's Perseverance Touches Down Safely in Search of Life," *The Guardian*, February 19, 2021, https://www.theguardian.com/science/2021/feb/18/nasa-perseverance-rover-mars-lands-life.

64 Natasha Riebe, "Edmonton Council Approves Zero Tax Increase Next Year," *CBC News*, December 11, 2020, https://www.cbc.ca/news/canada/edmonton/city-council-1.5838247.

65 To Do Canada, "Fun Things to Do in Edmonton Area During COVID-19 Alberta Reopening Phase," *To Do Canada*, June 15, 2020, https://www.todocanada.ca/tourist-activities-attractions-and-parks-open-in-edmonton-area-during-covid-19-alberta-reopening-phase/.

66 Jordan Omstead, "Edmonton's Mandatory Mask Bylaw to End on July 1 After City Council Vote," *CBC News*, June 25, 2021, https://www.cbc.ca/news/canada/edmonton/edmonton-mask-bylaw-expire-stage-3-1.6079789.

67 Emily Mertz, "Edmonton Election 2021: Amarjeet Sohi Elected Mayor," *Global News*, October 18, 2021, https://globalnews.ca/news/8266564/edmonton-election-2021-mayor-amarjeet-sohi/.

68 Lisa Johnson, "Alberta Election 2023: UCP Wins Majority Government, but Loses Key Seats," *Edmonton Journal*, May 29, 2023, https://edmontonjournal.com/news/politics/alberta-election-2023-voters-elect-new-premier.

69 Cameron MacCuish, "Meet the Mayoral Candidates Running in Edmonton's 2025 Municipal Election," *CBC News*, September 26, 2025, https://www.cbc.ca/news/canada/edmontonedmonton-mayoral-candidates-election-1.7643598.

70 "Recap: Liberals Hold Edmonton Centre, Conservatives Pick Up Griesbach, Rural Sweep for Tories," *Edmonton Journal*, April 28, 2025, https://edmontonjournal.com/news/local-news/live-albertans-vote-in-2025-federal-election.

71 "Why Are Wildfires So Common Now?," University of Calgary, accessed March 2, 2026, https://ucalgary.ca/sustainability/mobilizing-alberta/climate-action-blogs/why-are-wildfires-so-common-now.

72 Taylor Lambert, "A History of Cuts to Alberta's Firefighting Budget, Explained," *CBC News*, May 11, 2023, https://www.cbc.ca/news/canada/edmonton/a-history-of-cuts-to-alberta-s-firefighting-budget-explained-1.6838994.

73 "Much of Alberta, Saskatchewan Under a Blanket of Wildfire Smoke, Air Quality Warnings," *CBC News*, September 2, 2025, https://globalnews.ca/news/11389227/alberta-saskatchewan-wildfire-smoke-air-quality-warnings/.

74 Lauren Boothby, "More Than 700 Trees at Risk in Edmonton's Hawrelak Park Renewal: Report," *Edmonton Journal*, April 25, 2023, https://edmontonjournal.com/news/local-news/more-than-700-trees-at-risk-in-edmontons-hawrelak-park-renewal-report.

75 Natasha Riebe, "Patio Permit Fees, Cuts to Arts and Sports Groups on List as Edmonton Looks to Trim Budget," *CBC News*, February 21, 2024, https://www.cbc.ca/news/canada/edmonton/patio-permit-fees-cuts-to-arts-and-sports-groups-on-list-as-edmonton-looks-to-trim-budget-1.7121888.

76 "How Much Would You Pay for the Arts?," *CBC News*, November 12, 2024, https://www.cbc.ca/news/canada/edmonton/how-much-would-you-pay-for-the-arts-1.7381569.

77 "Letters Sept. 11: Stop Coddling Alberta's Anti-Vaxxers," *Edmonton Sun*, September 11, 2021, https://edmontonsun.com/opinion/letters/letters-sept-11-stop-coddling-albertas-anti-vaxxers.

78 "Airline Required to Compensate Families of Flight PS752 Victims, Ontario Court Rules," *CBC News*, August 11, 2025, https://www.cbc.ca/news/canada/toronto/airline-required-to-pay-families-of-flight-ps752-ontario-court-rules-1.7605996.

79 Hanna Alberga, "The World Has Moved On. But Those Who Lost Loved Ones to COVID-19 Feel Stuck in Time," *CBC News*, March 5, 2025, https://www.cbc.ca/news/canada/montreal/covid-19-deaths-five-years-later-1.7474989.

80 "Alberta COVID Babies Are Now Off to Kindergarten," *Global News*, August 28, 2025, video, 2 mins., 9 sec., https://globalnews.ca/video/11355071/alberta-covid-babies-are-now-off-to-kindergarten.

81 Crawford Kilian, "COVID-19 Is Six Today. What We've Learned," *The Tyee*, December 31, 2025, https://thetyee.ca/Analysis/2025/12/31/COVID-Six-What-Learned/.

Photo Credit: Yulia Skogoreva

Nisha Patel was the eighth Poet Laureate of the City of Edmonton and a Canadian Individual Poetry Slam champion. Nisha holds an MA from Queen's University and an MFA from UBC. She lives and writes from her home in Edmonton with her partner, fellow author and poet Matthew James Weigel. ***nishapatel.ca***